Who Were the Martyrs of Wigtown?

The Story of the Two Margarets

Lindsay Banks

First Published in 2023 by Lindsay Banks
Edited by Temple Woman Publishing
Front cover artwork by Harvey Mayson
Funding provided by DG Unlimited

Copyright © Lindsay Banks 2023

Lindsay Banks has asserted her right to be identified as the Author of this Work which has been asserted in accordance with the Copyright, Designs and Patent Act 1988 and Intellectual Property (Copyright and Related Rights) (EU Exit) (Amendment etc) Regulations 2019.

All rights reserved. No part of this book may be reproduced, or stored in a retrieval system, in any form or by any means, without the prior permission in writing of the author, with the exception of a reviewer who may quote brief passages or quotes.

ISBN: 978-1-7394573-0-3

From the Author

This book was inspired by a visit to the Martyrs of Wigtown stake in Wigtown, south-west Scotland, a small town also known as 'The Book Town'.

I was visiting the area in the summer of 2022 and, having visited the Martyr's Stake and wanted to discover more about these two women who had been killed. I couldn't find anything except for a plaque by the footpath briefly describing the martyrs names and the reason they were killed.

Further up the hill, in the churchyard, lay their gravestones which offered no further explanation as to who these women actually were. I wanted to know their story, who they were as women and why they had chosen to stand up for themselves at a time when they knew that the ultimate penalty would be death.

There are, within the many resources I have read, various versions of Margaret Lachlane's name. She was referred to as Lauchlison in the book 'The Wigtown Martyrs,' 1869, by Rev Archibald Stewart. I, however, will refer to her as Margaret Lachlane and I will distinguish between both Margarets by the initial letter of their surnames – Margaret L and Margaret W.

Some people believe that the martyrs were never actually killed and that it was a story made up to put fear into Covenantors around Scotland who, at the time, were growing in number and rebelling against the King and the system. However, if they were killed for their beliefs, these women deserve to have their stories told. My hope is that I have done justice to them and to their story in this book.

What follows is fiction based on the available facts.

Lindsay Banks

Contents

From the Author iii

Contents v

Acknowledgements 7

Chapter One 9
  Background 9

Chapter Two 17
  Summer 2022 17

Chapter Three 21
  11 May 1685- Margaret Wilson 21

Chapter Four 29
  Margaret Lachlane 29

Chapter Five 45
  The Betrayal - February 1685 45

Chapter Six 53
  The Killing of the two Margarets 53

Resources 67

About the Author 69

The Martyrs of Wigtown

Acknowledgements

I would like to thank the following people:

- D&G Unlimited for funding this book;
- My editor, and Director of Temple Woman Publishing, June Russell-Alexander, for helping me get this book published;
- Local artist, Harvey Mayson (also known as @ecoarts), for providing the artwork for the book cover;
- Susan, for her guidance and support during the writing process;
- Eva for her friendship and support
- Joe for being supportive and for encouraging me to follow my passion for writing
- Nicky at The Bookshop, Wigtown for lending me a book on the Martyrs of Wigtown, your support and encouragement
- Andy Hemingway also known as @darkgalloway on Twitter for allowing me to use his photos within the book; and
- The numerous other people I have spoken to about this book and who have supported me.

The Martyrs of Wigtown

Chapter One
Background
Scotland during the 16th and 17th century

In order to understand the story of the Martyrs of Wigtown, a brief history of Scotland and England during the early 1600s is essential.

Politics and religion were significant contributors to the conflict and contention of the time, which gave rise to the rebels - the Covenanters.[1] Societal, political and religious tensions had been rising steadily in Scotland culminating in the killing years of the late 1600s. The period 1679 to 1688, was a bleak time for the Covenanters.

In 1560, the Church of Scotland became Presbyterian[2]. Regulations for church government was established later during that year and ten ecclesiastical districts created. During the 16th century there was a Protestant Reformation. The Protestant Reformation was a religious reform movement that swept through Europe in the 1500s. It resulted in the creation of a branch of Christianity called Protestantism, a name used collectively to refer to the many religious groups that

---
[1] Covenanters were members of a 17th-century Scottish religious and political movement, who supported a Presbyterian Church of Scotland and the primacy of its leaders in religious affairs..
[2] Presbyterian means belonging or relating to a Protestant church which is governed by a body of official people all of equal rank.

separated from the Roman Catholic Church due to differences in doctrine[3] The Catholic Church resisted those wanting to reform and several different movements splintered from the Church and bore different dominations of Christianity, one of those being Presbyterianism. King James VI, King of Scotland from 1566-1625, had reached a compromise that leaned more towards an Episcopalian Church[4] government with a Calvinist theology[5].

Following the death of King James VI death, on 27 March 1625, King Charles I succeeded to the throne and he imposed Anglicanism[6] and Erastian[7] state control over the church. The English Parliament was not in favour of the King's actions and, fearing that Irish Catholics would lend their support to the Royalist army to further enforce the King's regime, it sought support from the Scots, namely, the Presbyterian Covenanters. However, the much-needed support was promised by the Covenanters on the condition that their ideologies would be adopted in England. A National Covenant was

---

[3] Source-National Geographic
[4] Of or advocating government of a Church by Bishops
[5] Calvinism is a major branch of Protestantism based on the works of John Calvin. It emphasises the sovereignty of God and the authority of the Bible.
[6] Anglicanism is another branch of Christianity based on their Christian faith on the Bible, traditions of the apostolic church, apostolic succession ("historic episcopate"), and the writings of the Church Fathers.[
[7] Thomas Erastus was the man behind the term Erastian. He had written over 75 theses on how the state should punish individuals and not the church. An Erastian state advocates the supreme authority of the state in church matters

drawn up and, although it did not explicitly name Presbyterianism, it did allow for preservation of the reformed religion in Scotland, Presbyterianism. The Scots travelled to England and fought in the First Civil War, defeating the Royalist army. Charles I was later executed in 1649.

In 1649, Charles II then became King of Scotland and was persuaded by the Presbyterians to sign the National Covenant. The Battle of Worcester took place in 1651. King Charles II had believed that his alliance with the Scottish Presbyterian Covenanters and his signing of the Solemn League and Covenant would encourage English Presbyterians to support him against the English Independent faction which had grown in power over the last few years[8].

In 1658, Charles II fled to mainland Europe after being defeated by Oliver Cromwell in the Battle of Worcester. Oliver Cromwell became the dictator of England, Scotland and Ireland until his death in 1658. In that same year, after Cromwell's death, Charles II returned from exile and declared the National Covenant unlawful and, in doing so, broke all ties with the Scottish Presbyterians. This was seen as an act of betrayal resulting in increased tension.

In 1661, the Recissary Act effectively nullified any and all legislation made since 1633. Over 400 church

---

[8] Source- Wikipedia

ministers were forced to abandon their posts in the churches and bishops were restored into the Church of Scotland.

In 1662, the Abjuration Act[9] formally rejected the National Covenant of 1638 and the Solemn League and Covenant of 1643[10] as being against the fundamental laws of the kingdom. Under the Abjuration Act, anyone taking public office was required to take the Oath of Abjuration and, in doing so, make a declaration that they would reject the Covenants and not take up arms against the King. This effectively excluded most Presbyterians from taking public office and led to civil unrest in Scotland.

The government alternated between persecution and toleration and, in 1663, declared dissenting church ministers as 'seditious persons' and imposed heavy fines on those who failed to attend the parish churches of the "King's curates". In 1666, around 800 Covenantors from Galloway, Scotland, marched on Edinburgh and were defeated at the Battle of Rullion Green. a brief revolt by Covenanter dissidents against the Scottish government. It had been sparked by opposition to the restoration of Episcopalianism in the Church of Scotland. A Covenanter army under Colonel James

---

[9] A formal rejection of the National Covenant of 1638 and the Solemn League and Covenant of 1643.

[10] a civil agreement by the English Parliamentarians, who needed military allies, but the Scots considered it a guarantee of their religious system. It was signed throughout England and Scotland.

Wallace was defeated by a government force led by Tam Dalyell of the Binns. Around 85 prisoners were taken and tortured; 33 were executed and the remainder transported to Barbados.

In 1667, the rebellious rising led to the replacement of the Duke of Rothes as King's Commissioner by John Maitland, 1st Duke of Lauderdale who followed a more conciliatory policy. The Duke of Rothes had been considered overzealous in his persecution of the Covenantors. Letters of Indulgence were issued in 1669, 1672 and 1679, allowing evicted ministers to return to their parishes if they agreed to avoid politics. A number returned to their parishes but over 150 refused, while many Episcopalians were alienated by the compromise. The outcome was a return to religious persecution; preaching at a conventicle[11] was made punishable by death, while attendance attracted severe sanctions.

In 1674, heritors and masters were made responsible for the 'good behaviour' of their tenants and servants and, from 1677, they had to post bonds for those living on their land. In Scotland, landowners in each parish had responsibilities within that parish and were called 'heritors.' They were involved in the process to choose a new minister or schoolmaster and responsible for maintaining the church, manse and

---

[11] A conventicle is an unlawful religious meeting, typically of nonconformists

schoolhouse. They also had responsibilities towards making sure the minister had sufficient glebe land close to the manse – land on which he could grow a few crops and keep a few horses, cattle and sheep. Other responsibilities involved keeping the roads in good repair.

In May 1679, the assassination of Archbishop Sharp by Covenanter radicals led to a revolt that ended at the Battle of Bothwell Bridge in June 1679. It was fought between government troops and militant Presbyterian Covenanters. A large number of Covenanters were killed or arrested and shipped off to the colonies. The estimate for how many were killed ranges from 7-700 and around 1200 were taken prisoner. All those who had taken part on the Covenanter side of the battle were declared rebels and traitors and the repression during this period has become known as "the Killing Time" in Covenanter histories. Several of the rebels remained in arms and became known as the Cameronians after Richard Cameron, their leader.

In 1680, Michael Cameron gave a speech, known as the Sanquhar Declaration, in the presence of his brother, the Covenanter leader Richard Cameron and was accompanied by twenty armed men in the public square of Sanquhar, Scotland. They disavowed allegiance to Charles II and the government of Scotland in the name of "true Protestant and Presbyterian interest" and in opposition to government interference in religious affairs.

In February 1685, Charles II died and King James VII was crowned King. He faced little opposition in Scotland. Scotland played a largely passive role in the revolution of 1688 until news of events in England and James' flight were followed by the collapse of the Scottish administration in late December. James VII forfeited the crown in 1689 and William and Mary became King and Queen of Scotland.

What follows is part fact and part fiction. A story of two brave women who were true to their beliefs, regardless of the consequences.

The Martyrs of Wigtown

Chapter Two
Summer 2022

Martha had only been in Scotland for a few weeks when she visited the Martyrs of Wigtown stake. She parked her car in a small, wooded area, on the edge of Wigtown and started to journey down the signposted path. She came across an information board dedicated to the Martyrs of Wigtown explaining who they were and why they were killed. Martha found herself angered by what she read. Martyrs? Why were they called Martyrs when all they had done was stand up for their beliefs and refuse to sign an oath to the King?

In search of more information, she made her way along the wooden, rickety pathway toward a grey, phallic stake; a concrete block about 10 feet high and shaped into a point. A small plaque at its base commemorated the two Martyrs; two women who had been drowned for standing up for their beliefs.

The stone stood as a solitary reminder of their life and death with the sea in the distance and the hills acting as a background drop for the atrocities which had occurred back in 1685.

Martha seethed with anger for several days after visiting the site and learning of the atrocity which took place so many centuries before. The women were victims who had been killed for standing up for themselves and their beliefs; killed for not agreeing with what the authorities did and said; killed by men who didn't have the balls to say, "You know what, this isn't okay"? They were killed by men who went along with the status quo.

What was the true story of these brave women? Why had they refused to sign an oath to the King?

Martha knew what it was like to stand up for herself against authorities. She had recently faced her own personal battle with the family court system and had been persecuted by having her children taken away from her because she chose to live her life as she wanted - a simple, wholesome, holistic, off-grid life that the system did not want to understand and would not agree with.

She empathised with these women. How could she not? They were killed for speaking their truth!

Who were the Martyrs of Wigtown? Why did they choose to stand up against the system in a time when they knew they may be killed for it? Martha decided to find out more about the women and their stories. There had to be more to them than a concrete phallic stone, an information board and their gravestones.

She started her research within the churchyard on the hill where their gravestones were situated. Within a fence lay their memorials.

The two headstones bore the following inscriptions:

*"Here lyes, Margaret Wilson, daughter of Gilbert Wilson
in Glenvernock, who was drowned anno 1685, aged 18
Let earth and stone still witness beare
There lyes a virgin martyr here
Murther'd for owning Christ supreame
Head of His Church and no more crime
But not abjuring presbytery
And her not owning prelacy
They her condemned by unjust law.
Of heaven nor hell they stood in aw
Within the sea ty'd to a stake
She suffered for Christ Jesus' sake.
The actors of this cruel crime
Were Lagg, Strachan, Winram and Grahame.
Neither young years nor yet old age
Could stop the fury of their rage.*

~~~

*Here lyes Margaret Lachlane,
Who was by unjust law sentenced
To die by Lagg, Strachan, Winrame,
And Grame, and tyed to a stake within the
Flood for her adherence to
Scotland's Reformation Covenant,
National and Solemn League,
Aged 63, 1685*

The Martyr's Stake, Wigtown
Photo c/o Andy Hemingway Dark Arts Galloway

Chapter Three
11 May 1685- Margaret Wilson

Margaret Wilson, aged 18 years, stood freezing in the cold, wearing the same white frock in which she had been arrested and tied to a wooden post with her feet in the cold sea. The crowd stood nearby silently looking on. She could see her friend, Margaret Lachlane, aged 63 years, in the distance, also tied to a post. The water was deep. Her friend was immersed up to her neck and the waves were lapping around her face. Amidst the horror of what was happening, she knew that she had to stand strong in her beliefs. She could not and would not back down now.

The man standing next to her looked at her with fury in his eyes. She pitied him. He had been weak; he had not been true to himself and his beliefs and, like everyone else, he had signed his life over to King James VII, a man he did not know and had never seen.

Margaret Wilson was one of the few who could not and would not comply. She knew her own mind and believed in her own powers. Some called it witchcraft; others magic but she knew her power was her inner knowing. She often foresaw events before they happened through her dreams. She intuitively knew which herbs and plants were needed for the sick. Her words acted as spells; that which she spoke aloud manifested into her reality. Her mother and grandmother also had this knowing and it been handed down to Margaret as a little girl. She had watched them in the kitchen, mixing their dried herbs together to make poultices and teas. She had listened to their words, not always sure of what they were saying but feeling the energy from them. Sometimes she saw things which others could not, invisible to the naked eye for others. Her mother had told her it was a gift but not one to be shared. She knew that not everyone was in a place to receive some of her visions and premonitions. What others couldn't see was just how powerful she was. She owed her life to Margaret Lachlane for teaching her this. She was a strong, powerful, human being. Others resented her for speaking her mind and standing in her power.

~~~

Margaret Wilson whispered under her breath, "The man who shalt kill me shalt suffer a life wanting for nowt but water." No-one heard her as her words were swept out to the sea by the strengthening wind. She could see the hills in the distance. She felt the cold seep deep into her bones. As the water rose above her knees, she knew this was the end. Her life was to end. She could not and would not repent, for that felt like a sin. She had dreamed of the afterlife many times and it was a beautiful place, far removed from the hell that others had threatened her with. Hell was here on Earth where she was being persecuted and murdered by weak men for following her heart and speaking her truth. She had had a couple of allies but unfortunately they were amongst the few.

She reconciled herself to the reality that her time had come. She did not dread it but welcomed it. She knew that one day someone would share her story and that her name would be remembered for centuries to come.

1683- Margaret Wilson

Margaret Wilson had grown up on Glenvernoch Farm on the outskirts of Newton Stewart, Scotland, with her father, Gilbert, and her mother, Beatrix. She never really felt that she fitted in with the rest of the family and she was regarded as 'the black sheep.' From an early age, she had a knowing. She had vivid dreams and instinctively knew when people were going to die. She shared these visions and premonitions with her parents but they didn't want to know. They feared that others in the village would think she was different and persecute her for it. So, she was told to be quiet and not to share her knowings with others. It was only in later years that she understood the reason for her parents' caution and fear.

The Wilsons were 'normal,' were accepted by the local community and would say what others wanted to hear and agree with the consensus of opinion. To the outside world, they were not rebels. However, in the privacy and safety of their home, Gilbert and Beatrix would speak in hushed tones about their true beliefs and feelings. Gilbert didn't agree with the local community. After a few cups of mead, he would become more vocal about his opinions to his wife and family and would question why he had to agree the enforced rules and regulations of the land. Margaret often sat on the stairs and listened to her father rant, with anger and frustration, about the goings on in their village and further afield.

At her age, Margaret wasn't old enough for her voice to be heard, to be acknowledged or considered. However, she listened intently to her father and took on board all of his opinions. It made sense to her, even as a child. Who was this King of whom they spoke? Why should a man who lived miles away make decisions about their lives? Little did her father know at the time that his own opinions and beliefs would later lead to the death of his daughter.

Margaret Wilson's family

Gilbert Wilson was a prosperous farmer. He had good soil and an abundance of crops, sheep and cows on his land. Married with his children, he was happy and content. A law-abiding citizen and with a strong faith in God, he was well-respected. Gilbert and his wife had brought their children up as well as they could but they struggled. They sympathised with the Presbyterians, yet they couldn't find it within themselves to stand up and refuse to go to church.

Their children, however, could and did. Gilbert wanted to align with his children but he knew that their entire livelihood, the farm, everything they held dear would be taken from them by the King's soldiers. Regardless of his true thoughts and beliefs, he complied and attended church, not just for his sake but for the safety and welfare of his family.

Within the family, division had arrived in the form of religion. It was a difficult time as the country was in conflict over religion and, more specifically, how the church was structured to manage the people in the towns and villages across the UK. Which structure was best to follow? Presbyterianism or Episcopalian? Although people had a choice as to which religion they chose to adhere to, there were consequences for those who did not choose the religion most favoured by the King. Covenanters supported the Presbyterian church and did not adhere to the laws of the land. They did not attend church and chose instead to worship God in the countryside with other likeminded people. It was a dangerous and challenging time.

Gilbert was well aware of the repercussions of being a Covenanter. Several of his children were Covenantors and several weren't. He was not, therefore, best placed to stand up against the imposed laws. He was tired and was uncertain if this was a battle that he could fight. Physically, his work as a farmer was challenging and he would often fall into bed every night exhausted. His children, on the other hand, were physically well and active. He admired them. They had stamina and fight in them. The absence of some of Gilbert's children from church on a Sunday did not go unnoticed. People began to gossip and ask questions. Rumours spread that Margaret and two of her siblings were Covenanters and it wasn't long until the soldiers found out and began to harass Gilbert but he refused to tell them his children's whereabouts.

Margaret, her brother and younger sister, who was only thirteen, attended the conventicles held in the countryside. They would go along to listen to the prayers and sermons and meet with other Covenanters. Their father, unfortunately, had been forced by the authorities to disown them so they had fled to nearby caves in the Galloway Hills. Margaret did not blame her father as she understood that the authorities would have burned down his farm and taken everything he and her mother had worked hard for. This was how the authorities tried to stamp out alternative religious beliefs and any acts of rebellion. No-one was permitted to speak out against the King or refuse to attend church.

Margaret didn't believe that God could only be found and praised in a building. If God was everywhere, surely it didn't matter if they were praying in a field or in a church. These musings often went through her mind as she walked through the countryside, listening to the sounds of the birds in the trees.

~~~

Gilbert sat outside the farmhouse looking out into the hills. His wife, Beatrix, brought him a cup of mead. His mind was not often far from his three children, hiding away in the hills, hiding away because they couldn't bring themselves to go to church. He didn't blame them. He didn't want to go to church either. However, his livelihood, his family's farm and the rest of his family depended on him. He couldn't take them to the hills to live in hiding forever. He wasn't in a position to stand by his beliefs. Every night he prayed that his children would be safe, that they wouldn't be captured, and he asked God to protect them. At a time when soldiers were regularly looting farms and killing people, it was easier to stay silent. To keep quiet and carry on as if everything was normal. His heart was heavy and his mind full.

~~~

The Martyrs of Wigtown

Chapter Four
Margaret Lachlane

Margaret Lachlane was a widow, living about a mile west of Wigtown, a remote and scenic spot. Her late husband had been a carpenter and had left her with a small farm to manage. She had always been a strong-minded woman of independent thought and beliefs. Her life was uneventful for the most part until one fateful day when she received a message from God.

On that day, she decided not to attend church. Her faith in God was strong and her God had spoken to her and told her that worship did not require attendance at a church. Her God was wherever she chose to worship him. She listened to God's message, heard it, and received it and stopped attending the local church.

Her absence was noticeable. Questions were asked about her sudden departure from the church. Accusations were made about her belief and faith in God. However, God had told Margaret that faith and prayer were all that was needed to worship Him, regardless of the location. She didn't care what people thought or what they believed, for she had been visited by Christ and told it was not necessary to pray together in one building, for prayer alone was enough, no matter where one may be.

She was a woman who stood firm in her beliefs and values and was not swayed by the majority.

Margaret missed her husband, John Mulligen. She had a farm to run and an income to make for the upkeep of the farm and herself. She had no time for local gossip. Her farm was her livelihood and now depended solely on her. Only she could manage it and earn her keep.

Often, it was tough but she persevered as she raised her chickens, cows and sheep to sell at market. She was also fascinated by herbs and loved to forage. She would often go out into the fields to find what was lying in abundance in the land. Mugwort, Heather, Sage and Rosemary were dried in her kitchen. Mushrooms were picked and dried when they were in season. She knew exactly when the various herbs, plants and berries would appear and what to do with them. Her grandmother had shown her the ways of old; how to make teas and tinctures, natural remedies, herbal concoctions, not just for her but for those around her.

Margaret's home became known as a safe space for wanderers in Scotland, especially to the Covenanters, who had chosen to worship God in the fields around the towns and villages. Hers was an open house and others, who had similar beliefs and values to her, would call upon her for shelter and sustenance. The wanderers would speak to each other in passing and knew that they would not be turned away if they knocked on Margaret's door. Many had been forced to flee from their homes and towns for standing true in their own beliefs and values. They faced arrest for not attending church. Many fled and became wanderers, travelling from town to town, village to village, trying to find their kin.

The meeting of the two Margarets

One day, a young woman came to Margaret Lachlane's home. She was of pleasant appearance, with long red curly hair and wearing a shawl wrapped around her head and shoulders. Dressed in a long brown skirt and sturdy boots, she looked a little weathered and cold. Margaret Lachlane invited her into her home and made her a warm drink. The young woman wrapped her hands around the cup to warm them.

"I have heard tales and stories of you," the young woman began. "Many who I have met have spoken of you and your worship. I am of similar belief to you yet I am finding it increasingly difficult to not abide by the rules. My family are struggling because of me. My father, who is seen as a law-abiding citizen, is being tormented and accused of covering for me not attending church. However, it is not only me but also my younger sister and brother who feel this way. Can you help us?"

Margaret Lachlane was not entirely sure how she could help this young woman. She had had wanderers call to her home before but none had every asked for help in this way. "I will," she heard herself say. She spoke the words before she even had time to think. She knew that it was a crime to offer refuge to the wanderers and that, if caught, she would be arrested. The King's soldiers had already robbed and pillaged her farm several times but had never caught anyone staying with her. However, her duty was to God, not to the soldiers, and she would help this young woman as God would wish her to do..

Margaret Wilson had walked for hours to reach the house of Margaret Lachlane. She had heard stories of how this woman was conducting her own sermons in her house for those who did not want to attend church, for those who did not believe in the Anglican rites. She was not persuaded by her father or her family that it was the right thing to do. She had her own beliefs and values and held firm in her decision.

She was only seventeen years old but she was headstrong as her father, Gilbert, who was a stubborn man but he still went to church and was respected in the local area. She wanted to meet someone like her, someone who didn't agree with the rules and laws of the land. She hoped she would find some comfort in meeting Margaret Lachlane.

Little did she know that this initial meeting would lead to her death.

The Sanquhar Declaration

In 1680, Margaret Wilson heard of a man by the name of Richard Cameron, a great leader in the Covenanter's circle. She wanted to see this man for herself and had heard that he and his brother would be in Sanquhar.

Situated by the River Nith, Sanquhar, had become a destination for Covenanters to gather and speak. Surrounded by hills and beautiful scenery, it was halfway between Ayr and Dumfries and the only major town in a large area. It was well known for people to go to Sanquhar to proclaim their testimonies on a variety of political movements. It was a hotbed of unrest.

It would involve a few days' travelling to get there but Margaret wanted to hear what Richard Cameron had to say. Her brother would accompany her whilst her sister would stay with friends. They would be going as representatives of the area and they wanted to offer their full support to Richard and the other protestors.

On 22 June 1680, Margaret and her brother arrived in Sanquhar. They tethered their horses in a field on the outskirts of the town and continued on foot to the main street. A crowd of perhaps 20 people had gathered around the town's mercat cross - the market cross where historically the right to hold a regular market was granted by the monarch or the bishop.

The crowd sang a psalm before Michael Cameron, brother of Richard, gave his speech. He called for war against King Charles II and denounced him as a tyrant. There was much cheering from the crowd and waving of weapons. Margaret could see local villagers watching from a distance. She observed the two Cameron brothers; Michael spoke with confidence and passion while Richard stood quietly by his side. Michael recited the Sanquhar declaration, calling for war on Charles II and the exclusion of the Roman Catholic, James - Duke of York. Richard then spoke. His voice surprised her. Calm and steady, he spoke of the previous year's battles of Bothwell Bridge and Drumclog and the assassination of Archbishop Sharpe who had supported the governance of the bishops. A second assassination attempt by the Presbyterians ultimately killed him.

When Richard and his brother had finished speaking, Margaret and her brother invited them to come and speak to the people who lived in Newton Stewart and the surrounding areas. Margaret also wanted to introduce them to her friend, Margaret Lachlane. The brothers happily agreed that they would travel to Newton Stewart later that year. As they said their farewells to travel home, Margaret instinctively knew that she would not see Richard again. She was unsure of his fate but felt that whatever was to happen was all part of God's plan.

As often happened, Margaret dreamed vividly that night. She could see Richard Cameron, an ambush and blood being spilled. She awoke with a start, her heart beating fast, hoping that this was not to be. That dream stayed with her throughout the following day. What was to become of Richard? What would happen if he was no longer delivering sermons across the Southwest of Scotland? Who would lead the Covenanters to their victory? Michael or someone else? Although Michael was a great orator, he did not have the skills of a great leader. He did not make time to get to know people and listen to them. She knew that somehow, she had to keep the words that the Camerons had spoken alive in her heart and her soul. As a woman, she wasn't permitted to lead the conventicles or to speak publicly but she could speak to those that she lived with.

Determined to make a difference, over the next few weeks, she confided in trusted friends about witnessing and listening to the Cameron brothers' speeches. Her words seemed to instill courage in those around her. They were not alone. There were others around Scotland who shared their beliefs.

Unfortunately, before long, news came that Richard Cameron had been killed in an ambush, as she foresaw. It was said that on 22 July, he and his men had been ambushed by Government dragoons and it was rumoured that, before his head and hands were severed from his body, he spoke these final fatal words:

"Now, let us fight it out to the last: for this is the day I have longed for, and the day I have prayed for, to die fighting against our Lord's avowed enemies?"

Margaret wept when she heard the news of Richard's death. She questioned what his bravery and strength had achieved and how any rebellion against the King could succeed. She knelt down on the wet grass and prayed to God, not only for Richard's soul but also for all those who refused to deny their beliefs and swear allegiance and obedience to an English King. She vowed that, should she ever happen upon this King, she would curse him. Her friend, Margaret Lachlane, had been teaching her about the ways of the witches. Spell casting was something that intrigued her and she had become quite skilled in the practice.

When she had finished praying, she made a commitment to God. "Whatever path you have chosen for me, I shall honour it and stand with courage and loyalty. I shall never deny my faith."

In that moment, her fate was sealed. She had made a promise to God that she would keep forever – until her dying day.

Another leader did come along and take Richard Cameron's place; a man named James Renwick. He was a man who fought for what was right, who followed his heart.

Following the Camerons' declaration, he too travelled to Sanquhar to share his testimony. He gathered the troops and, as over 100 armed men descended into Sanquhar, the local townsfolk fled in fear. James Renwick shared his testimony. He made his declaration and the Sanquhar Declarations set in motion the basis of religious freedom in Scotland.

~~~

Margaret Lachlane sat by the fire listening to the younger woman share her story. She and her brother had travelled to Sanquhar to listen to Richard Cameron and his brother, Michael. Margaret Lachlane had had a vision. She had become accustomed to her visions over the years. She had prophesied many things since she was a young girl; the passing of her father, then her mother and lastly her husband. She knew when death was upon someone.

Now, before her was young Margaret Wilson, sharing the story of her own vision. The older woman had initially believed that predicting someone's passing was a curse. However, over the years, she had come to accept that she had the gift of a seer and, for her own safety, she confided in only a few trusted people. She knew things that others did not and she saw this as an advantage. She knew always to keep one eye on the enemy and the other on her friends. She knew what the enemy was planning and where they were. She knew their weaknesses. Knowledge was power and, with her gift of foresight, she knew much more than others.

As the young woman recounted her vision, Margaret Lachlane knew she was to take this girl under her wing and teach her about her practices and sermons. She could see much of herself in this young woman who was lost, not knowing who to speak to or turn to. She had turned to God for answers and, although the messages weren't always direct, she always found guidance and comfort in prayer

Margaret Lachlane had been naturally guided to working with the land on which she now lived. She worked with the abundance of berries, herbs and leaves from which she made teas and poultices. Often, locals would seek her out for herbal remedies. Sometimes, there would be a quiet knock on her door in the evening; sometimes a subtle nod in the street and a hushed word. She acknowledged their requests and passed her remedies to them discreetly. She covered them with a blanket so no one could see what she was carrying in her homemade weaved basket. A cross hung above her door; a symbol of faith. Lord knows, she was being tested in her faith right now.

However, like Margaret Wilson, she was steadfast in her views and beliefs. She liked the young woman and invited her to stay the evening. She had a small barn outside which was warm enough; a couple of blankets and a hot cup of herbal tea would see Margaret through the night. She would speak with her in the morning after she had a good night's sleep.

Margaret Wilson woke up to the sound of cows mooing and sheep bleating. For a moment, she forgot where she was before remembering that she was at Margaret Lachlane's home. She shook the hay from her dress and walked to the farmhouse to speak with the older woman who was stoking the fire as she walked in. The kitchen was small but quaint. Herbs and flowers hung to dry from the rafters. How young Margaret yearned for a kitchen of her own to prepare and cook food for herself and her family. Alas, this wasn't her path now. Hers was to stand up against injustice and for truth. This path had been chosen for her and she had come to accept and feel easier with it.

Margaret Lachlane put a pan of water over the fire to heat. There was a comfortable silence between the two women as they gazed at the flames crackling in the hearth. The older Margaret was around her grandma's age. She was short, well rounded and with a gaze that could kill if you crossed her. She didn't look like a typical 'rebel.' "They come in all shapes and sizes," she thought. She knew it was risky to have travelled to Margaret Lachlane's home, let alone to have stayed in her house but she was seeking the elder woman's guidance.

Margaret Wilson already knew in her heart that she was meant to lead. But how? How was she to lead? Margaret Lachlane looked at her as if reading her thoughts. "You lead from your heart," she said. "When you stand strong in your own beliefs and values others will follow. It is not the easiest path you have chosen and one of great sacrifice. Choosing to leave behind your family and your home to seek that which others fear takes great courage. Your name will be remembered forever for the path you have chosen and the course you will take. It will not be easy but I think you already know that. Many people refuse to be slaves, to be told what to do and what to believe. They are looking to you for guidance on how they can be free of the tyranny that currently surrounds us."

Margaret Wilson considered the elder woman's words. In her heart, she knew she was right. She agreed to attend the conventicles with Margaret Lachlane when she could. Unfortunately, travelling in large groups drew unwanted attention so they would travel in smaller groups. Together, they were bound to protect the Covenanters as best they could. Externally, the battles and wars that were raging were led by men. What was missing was female guidance and leadership. They could still lead by gathering the hearts of men and women alike who refused to bow to the tyranny. Their friendship was cemented in their joint passion and beliefs.

As the younger Margaret rode back over the hills to what was now her home, she thought about the words Margaret Lachlane had said to her. She knew this woman was going to be a huge part of her life; she wasn't sure how but that same knowing that had come with Richard's passing now washed over her again. When she arrived back home, for what else could she call it, the others were eager to hear of her journey and this other "Margaret." That night, as they sat around the fire, she recounted the events of the previous days and what Margaret Lachlane had told her. Several of the group wanted to travel to meet this woman and connect with other Covenanters. So, they agreed that the following week they would go, only four of them, including Margaret Wilson who would guide them to their destination. As the days slowly rolled by, all was quiet in their home.

Theirs was a makeshift abode. They had found an abandoned barn in the hills which they slept in when it was cold. As the summer months came, they slept outside under the stars. It was quiet, save for the birds in the trees, the deer hooves clattering past in the evenings and the gentle sound of cows and sheep from nearby fields. Nobody knew they were there. It felt safe. The siblings slept under blankets on a bed of hay, holding each other close for warmth and comfort. Their home was basic yet they had everything they needed.

The women foraged the plants and berries from the land, whilst the men hunted and brought back their offerings for all to share. There was a loch nearby, plentiful with fresh fish which also made for a filling supper. The group ranged in ages from little children to elderly men and women. A group of refugees, they had been forced to flee their homes for fear of death. Some of them fled to save their families and had nowhere else to go. To hide a Covenanter in your house was not only frowned upon but also meant jail penalties or worse. It wasn't worth it, so they came together where there was safety in numbers. They knew there were other groups around Scotland who lived in the same way. Tales would often be told of great leaders standing up to deliver sermons against the King and refusing to swear the Abjuration Oath.

Agnes Wilson, Margaret's sister, was only fifteen years old and yet had fled into the hills alongside her brother and sister. She looked up to her older siblings and, when they had decided to join the Covenanters, she joined them with no understanding of how difficult this life would be. She sometimes dreamed of being back at home on the farm with her father, mother and siblings. She had always had a warm bed and food to eat. They weren't a rich family but they weren't poor. Her parents would always ensure that the children were fed before they fed themselves. Her childhood had been busy, helping out on the farm, and she remembered a lot of joy and laughter amongst the children as they ran freely around the farm.

She wasn't the youngest in the group; there were other Covenanters who had fled with their children. Although she was fifteen and still a child herself, she found herself acting like a surrogate mother to some of the little ones. They came to sit with her under the trees and she told them stories. She plaited the girls' hair and played with them. Often their parents were hunting, cooking or mending. She didn't mind. It reminded her of home and, although these children were not her blood brothers and sisters, it didn't matter to her. She loved spending time with them.

January 1685

All parishioners in the area were forced to sign the Abjuration Oath. As the Wilson siblings were currently living in the hills, none of them signed it. They effectively became fugitives.

The Martyrs of Wigtown

Chapter Five
The Betrayal - February 1685

The two Wilson daughters had travelled by way of Carrick, Galloway and Nithsdale before venturing to Wigtown to stay with the elder Margaret.

It was during this visit with Margaret Lachlane that they were betrayed by a local man called Baillie Patrick Stewart. Patrick had visited Margaret's house several times and had built a trusting relationship with the women. He had declared himself a loyal supporter of the Covenanters but, in truth, he had ulterior motive

Baillie Patrick Stewart was a man who had not reached what he felt was the level of recognition he deserved in Wigtown and wanted to be regarded as a man of great importance. He had hatched a plan to befriend these women and gain their trust, slowly, before betraying them and being paid handsomely for his efforts. He would not only be rewarded financially but also his standing within the town would be raised significantly. The Covenanters were a menace to society; they were rebels and outlaws. They felt as if they were above the law and he was determined to teach them a lesson.

When he invited both Margaret and Agnes Wilson to his home, they willingly accepted. He poured some wine not long after their arrival and invited them to drink to the King's health. They politely declined his request. "Traitors!" he shouted. At that moment, the doors burst open and soldiers stormed in. The girls were manhandled out of the house and taken away. They were cast into confinement in the 'thieves hole,' a stone-walled cell inside the Wigtown tollbooth - now the Wigtown County Building. It was only six feet wide and four feet across with one tiny window which let in some daylight and a smaller window in the large bolted wooden door. There were no comforts in the grey, cold and dark cell. Sitting on the cold floor of the confinement cell, holding onto each other for warmth, Margaret reassured her younger sister that all would be well, that they would pray to God and He would give them the strength and courage to overcome the situation in which they found themselves.

Early in their confinement, they were questioned as to why they had been travelling in Wigtownshire and they were asked for their travel papers. Upon taking the Abjuration Oath, people were given a piece of paper which allowed them to travel between different parishes. The Wilson girls, having never taken the Oath, could not provide the papers. They were left in the thieves' hole with basic rations whilst Baillie Patrick Stewart and Provost William Coltrane decided their fate.

The following day, Margaret Lachlane was thrown into the thieves' hole. After capturing Margaret Wilson and her sister, Baillie Patrick Stewart and his cohort had travelled to the elder Margaret's house to arrest her.

She was alone in the house at the time. She had also refused to take the Oath and had no travel papers to show. The women talked about their options and, in the end, they agreed to stand strong in their beliefs. They talked until the early hours before falling asleep on the cold floor.

Margaret Wilson dreamed of a woman with long, brown hair that night. She was looking out to sea and crying. Margaret was unsure as to why the woman was sad. In her dream, she approached the woman from behind and placed her hand on her shoulder. The woman had turned as she had felt a presence but could not see Margaret. She recounted her dream to Agnes and Margaret Lachlane. "A vision," the elder Margaret pronounced. "This woman in your dream will be very important to us, perhaps not now, but in the future."

They began to pray together, asking God for help and for a sign that would support them in their faith. One hour later, they were each dragged out and questioned about where their families were; if their families knew that they had not taken the Oath; and about other Covenanters. All three women refused to say anything. After a couple of hours of intense questioning and threats of torture, they were thrown back into the cell.

On 13 April 1685, the jury of the Assize[12] came together. Present were Laird of Lagg, Colonel David Graham, Major Windram, Captain Strachan, Provost Coltrane and Baillie McKeand. The women knew that there was no chance of true justice being served. These men were known for their stoical beliefs and had all signed the oath. They saw the women as rebels, as disobedient. They were not to be tolerated and must be taught a lesson – which they were determined to do. The two Margaret's and Agnes were charged with being at the Battle of Bothwell Bridge and attending conventicles. None of the charges could be proven. Once again, they were asked to take the Oath of Abjuration and, once again, they refused. Their execution date was set for 11 May and they were to be drowned in the Solway Firth.

Little did these men know that the women they were dealing with were magical. They could cast spells and curses. Although they had this knowledge, they had never used their words to intentionally harm another. They were both of kind heart and had used their spells to help others, not to curse them. Sitting in the cell, both Margarets felt anger and rage welling up within. Although they were accepting of their situation, they felt enraged at the injustice. The men who had chosen to arrest and persecute them would ultimately pay a price.

---

[12] A court which formally sat at intervals to administer the civil and criminal law

Curses would be cast, not only on them but also on their families and the generations to come. They did not need any candles or cauldrons in the prison cell. All they needed were their words and their strong intentions.

News had reached Gilbert that his daughters had been arrested and put in the thieves' hole in Wigtown. He knew he wouldn't be able to see them. After speaking with his wife, he decided to travel to Edinburgh to plead for them to be pardoned. He knew there would be a trial and hoped that he would be able to save his daughters from a dreadful fate. He wondered how life had come to this, where people were prosecuted for their beliefs. He himself had been harassed over the previous couple of years for having children who were effectively fugitives in the eyes of the law. His youngest was only fifteen, still a child herself. He could not bear to do nothing. Appealing to those in power was his only chance of saving them. Lord knows where his son was but, hopefully, he was free in the hills somewhere. He could not bear to think of his precious daughters being tried for a crime and being left to rot in prison, or worse, being killed. His mission was to save them and he prayed that he would make it to Edinburgh on time. Gilbert succeeded in receiving a pardon for both his daughters and, for a payment of £100, a huge sum at the time, he negotiated the release of his youngest daughter, Agnes.

"The Lords of his Majesties Privy Council doe hereby reprive the execution of the sentance of death pronunced by the Justices against Margret Wilson and Margret Lauchlison and discharges the magistrats of Edinburgh for putting of the said sentence to execution against them untill the forsaid day; and recomends the saids Margret Wilson and Margret Lauchlison to the "Lords Secretaries of State" to interpose with his most sacred Majestie for his royall remission to them."

Provost Coltrane, however, was a law unto himself and a man who would not go back on his word. He had promised the execution of these women to the local townsfolk and an execution was what they would have. He received the pardon from Edinburgh but pretended that he had not. He released the younger girl, Agnes. However, it was not in his best interests to release the other women as he wanted people to understand the consequences of refusing to abide by the laws of the land. To that end, he decided on a public execution to ensure that the people of Wigtown would see that the penalty for not abiding by the law was death.

He was a harsh man who did not tolerate disobedience of any kind. The law dictated that people must attend church and so it must be. There was money to be made in the church and if people did not attend then the church would suffer.

Provost Coltrane was a mead-swilling larger man who wanted power. He wanted to show the local people that he wasn't to be ignored or challenged. He was a Royalist and would do anything for the King. Woe betide anyone, be it woman or man, who would get in his way. His intention was clear. Kill the women and no more would be said. However, that wasn't to be.

The Martyrs of Wigtown

Chapter Six
The Killing of the two Margarets

As the two Margarets made their way from the prison cell down to the shore, many people came out to see them. Indeed, the streets were lined with local townsfolk. Some of the women stood silently, their heads bowed, hands pressed together, as if they didn't want to be there. Men stood with heads held high. Children ran amongst the adults with no understanding of what was happening.

One of the bystanders was James Heron. He was twenty years old, around the same age as the younger woman who he now watched walking down towards the sea. Many people around him were praying for the two women. Like the townsfolk, James was unsure of his feelings about this public execution of the two women. Although not a Covenanter himself, he did sympathise with them, having been forced to flee their homes and live in the hills. He himself had conversed with them many times and found them to be friendly and courteous. They happily told him the reasons why they refused to sign the Oath. They believed in freedom and didn't want to be forced to go to church when they believed God was everywhere. He could understand their point of view.

Margaret Lachlane and Margaret Wilson walked one behind the other; hands tied with rope, following the footsteps of the men. The crowd fell in line behind them. It was like a funeral procession except they were not yet dead. They were still very much alive.

The younger Margaret started uttering words under her breath that no one else could hear. She was praying. Praying to God for a peaceful death. Praying to God that those who had persecuted her may meet with untimely deaths. Cursing those who had brought her here. No one could hear her words - they would not have wanted to. Both women were accepting of their fate. They knew that, on this day, they would die. They both believed that this was God's will. Neither was willing to sacrifice their beliefs and values and this was the price they must pay. They did not cry. They did not shout or curse aloud. Quietly, they followed the group of men who had decided their fate.

Gilbert and his family stood amongst the crowd, watching their young daughter walking to her death. He had managed to save Agnes but not Margaret. His heart was broken. He was still proud of her for choosing to follow her heart and her beliefs but he was saddened that it had led to this. He was also financially ruined as it had cost him £100 to save Agnes; a bribe offered in exchange for his youngest daughter's life. His family now had nothing and were losing one child. They did not know where to go or what to do. They only knew that they could not stay at the farm. It had been ransacked after Margaret's arrest. Sheep and cows had been slaughtered and their home destroyed in the pursuit of other Covenanters. Despite no-one being found in their home, the farm was destroyed. They had to leave and start again. They had already packed their few belongings and would be leaving the following day. But, for now, they had come to say goodbye. As Margaret walked past, Gilbert could see her lips moving. She was muttering. "Probably praying," he thought. She looked up and, as she caught her father's eye, she smiled and gave a brief nod. He fought back the tears. This would be the last time he saw his daughter alive.

As they approached the water's edge, the women looked out to sea at the expanse and the sheerness of the sparkling water. If this was to be their fate, they were both willing to accept it. God would look after them. They had no fear and, as they looked at each other, a silent nod between them said, "This is what we must do. We accept our fate."

Two stakes had been erected, one for the elder Margaret and one for the younger. The elder Margaret was taken first and tied to the stake by a man named Bell. As the sea rose over her, she remained silent and accepting. Meanwhile, the men looked at the younger Margaret, wondering if she would she relent and comply or if she too would die at the stake. As the younger Margaret watched her friend succumbing to the rising tide, she made a vow to herself and to God, "I am not afraid of the destiny you have planned for me." She began to quietly sing the 25th Psalm.

To you, O Lord, I lift up my soul;
In you I trust, O my God. Do not let me be put to shame,
nor let my enemies triumph over me
No one whose hope is in you will ever be put to shame,
but they will be put to shame who are treacherous
without excuse
Show me your ways, O Lord, teach me your paths;
Guide me in your truth and teach me, for you are God
my Savior and my hope is in you all day long
Remember O Lord, your great mercy and love, for they
are from of old
Remember not the sins of my youth and my rebellious
ways, according to your love remember me, for you are
good, O Lord
Good and upright is the Lord; therefore he instructs
sinners in his ways
He guides the humble in what is right and teaches them
his way
All the ways of the Lord are loving and faithful for those
who keep the demands of his covenant
For the sake of your name, O Lord, forgive my inquiry,
though it is great
Who, then, is the man that fears the Lord? He will

instruct him in the way chosen for him
He will spend his days in prosperity and his descendants will inherit the land
The Lord confides in those who fear him; he makes his covenant known to them
My eyes are ever on the Lord, for only he will release my feet from the snare
Turn to me and be gracious to me, for I am lonely and afflicted
The troubles of my heart have multiplied, free from my anguish
Look upon my affliction and my distress and take away all my sins
See how my enemies have increased and how fiercely they hate me!
Guard my life and rescue me; let me not be put to shame, for I take refuge in you
May integrity and uprightness protect me, because my hope is in you

She finished singing and was silent for a moment before being dragged to the second stake which was slightly closer to the shore. Her hands were tied with rope around the stake. As the water rose above her head, she became frightened. She started singing again. Pulled out of the water, she was asked by her persecutors if she would pray for the King. "God save him as he will be saved," was her reply.

She refused, once again, to take the Abjuration Oath and her fate was sealed. She quietly cursed the men who were taking her life. As the water rose above young Margaret's head, she tried to hold her breath under the water but could only do so for a couple of minutes. She gasped for air; water filled her mouth, her throat and her lungs. She knew that this was the end in this lifetime. As the waves lapped around her body, she had a floating sensation. She could see her body tied to the stake. It was below her. The townsfolk and the men responsible for her death were standing at the water's edge chatting as if it was a normal day. She was dead but she could see them. She tried to scream, "I'm dead!" but no-one could hear her. The provost was gloating about their killings. "They needed to be killed," he said. "Some women don't know when they need to behave and toe the line." On hearing this, she thought, "I'm going to teach you a lesson." No one could see her or feel her so it was easy for her to move around. She knew that those involved in her own and Margaret Lachlane's passing would pay the price. Killing two innocent women would bring retribution to those involved.

She could see her father in the crowd. She moved towards him as he knelt, sobbing. He had tried so hard to keep his emotions in check but to no avail. Margaret placed her arms around him, holding him. For a moment, she thought he could feel her there. He looked up and straight into her eyes. Had he seen her? Perhaps. His head turned once more into his hands. She looked around the crowd and saw the faint outline of Margaret Lachlane in the distance. They walked towards each other and held hands. This was it. They were passing into the next world together knowing that their souls would carry on to another place.

The Martyr of Solway by John Everett Millais, 1871

After the drownings

Following the drownings of Margaret Lachlane and Margaret Wilson, life continued as normal for the people of Wigtown. Many of the Covenanters continued to hide in the hills. Gilbert and his family were bankrupt and chose to make their way to Ireland for a fresh start. The pain of losing their daughter in such a cruel way had taken its toll on Gilbert and his wife.

What of those involved in the actual persecution of the Martyrs? Nineteen years later, Baillie McKeand, who had sat on the jury and condemned the women to death reportedly said, *" the great grief of his heart that he should have sitting on the assize of these women, who were sentenced to die in this place in 1685 and yet it had been frequently his petition to God for repentance and forgiveness for the sin"* He had been plagued with guilt since the drownings. He hadn't wanted to kill these women but had been coerced into it by the Provost Coltrane.

Just before the older Margaret had passed, she had cast a curse on the Provost that he would receive retribution for what he had done to her and to Margaret Wilson. Provost Coltrane was visited by the daughter of Margaret Lachlane twenty-three years later with a message from her mother. She had a dream where her mother had appeared and *"bade her go and warn Provost Coltrane that he must shortly appear before*

God" Sometime later, the Provost rode to Stranraer to a meeting of Quarter Sessions and, whilst sitting at the court table, he was suddenly struck down with a lethargy. He was carried to his quarters, remained speechless and died on Saturday, 08 November 1708.

Bell, who had tied both women to the stake, also suffered later in life. When he had been asked how the women had behaved when the tide began to rise above them, he remarked, *" O, they just clepped roun' the stobs like partons an' aye prayed"* (They crawled round the stakes like crabs and I prayed). Bell's wife had a baby who was clepped, their fingers grew firmly together. All their children were born like this, perhaps as a result of a curse which had been passed onto their children by the two women.

Another man involved, and who seemed to get immense pleasure from their drownings, was a 'town's officer.' He had pressed the women's heads down with his halberd[13], crying *"There, tak' another drink 't, my herties."* For the rest of his days, this man suffered an unquenchable thirst. He would have to carry a huge pitcher everywhere with him. If he was by a stream, he would have to kneel down and take a sip. He even drank from filthy puddles. Men and women who once respected him turned away from him. The people of the

---

[13] A spear shaped point, small axe blade and a back spike, often curved. Carried by town officials and town guards

town who had sympathised with the women, and there were a few, believed he had dared the vengeance of Providence and, rather than wait until he reached the Pearly Gates on Judgement Day, he was now suffering.

The Martyrs' Legacy

An obelisk was erected in 1858 by a Mr James Todd where the two Margarets had passed away. He was the author of "The Fifty Years' Struggle of the Covenanters." It seemed ironic that once there was hatred and anger towards these women and yet two hundred years later they were being praised.

The legend of the Martyrs of Wigtown continues to raise questions. Did they really exist? Was this a plot to convince other Covenanters to comply? Whether it be truth or myth, the stories of these women deserve to be told and shared.

In the 21st century, more women are rising up and demanding that their stories be heard. Should we not offer that same space for the women who have gone before us? Should we not show respect and admire the women that chose to not conform or comply with unjust societal, political and religious dictats? Whether or not you believe that Margaret Lachlane and Margaret Wilson were drowned at the stake, they deserve to have their voices heard at last. None of us will ever know the definitive truth of what happened back then and, whilst this is not by any means a factual account, I hope I have done justice to the story of their lives, their strength of belief and their bravery in taking a stand against the injustice for which they were killed.

Martyr's Gravestones
Andy Hemingway aka @darkgalloway

Summer 2022

The story of the two Margarets floated around Martha's mind. She stood by the shore and vowed that she would share their story so that the manner of and reason for their deaths might be remembered - that they died for freedom. As she made this vow, she began to shiver as if someone had stood on her grave. She felt a hand on her shoulder although there was no one there. *"Yes,"* she heard someone say. It was a woman's voice. *"Share our story; it is time. As you are facing challenges around your own freedom now, this is a reminder to people of what can happen when those freedoms are denied. You were born to be free, not to abide by unjust laws and rules which restrict your freedom. Your soul is always free."*

With that, the pressure on Martha's shoulder lifted. She would share their story and encapsulate it in a book that could be read by others. Their voices were not heard in 1685 but they will be heard in 2023 and beyond.

They speak it oft in Scotland's homes
'Tis told in far-off lands
How in the bloom of youth she died
Upon the Solway sands
And souls are thrilled and hearts beat high
To hear the story told
How nobly she maintained her faith
In days that now are old
And how she kept her trust in God
And how she scorned the foe
And how she lived, and how she died
Two hundred years ago

Rev R. Riach Thom

A Final Word from the Author

Writing the story of Margaret Lachlane and Margaret Wilson has been an extraordinary and interesting journey. Visiting the Martyrs' cell where they were taken after arrest, the graves and the stakes are, for me, a stark reminder of what it means to stand up for your freedom and your beliefs. For thousands of years many women, and men, have been killed for speaking their truth, for refusing to abide by unjust laws and systems which deny people their true freedom. This is just one of thousands of stories.

When I first visited Wigtown, which is a beautiful town in Dumfries and Galloway and is also known as the book capital of Scotland, I was drawn to the stories of the Martyrs, their lives encapsulated on an information board.

Although hugely different in terms of gravity, I recognised parallels between what they endured and what I had recently experienced in the family court system. I chose to live a lifestyle that the system did not and would not understand. I was persecuted for my beliefs and sacrifices were made. I felt raw and angry at the injustice in my case when I visited the Martyrs' site at Wigtown. Writing this book felt like a constructive way to channel that anger while giving them a voice in the hope that it would inspire others to use their voices in today's world.

The Martyrs of Wigtown

Resources

Online Resources

Covenanting Pilgrimages and Studies A.B. Todd 1911

http://www.prca.org/books/portraits/margaret.htm
https://en.wikipedia.org/wiki/Solemn_League_and_Covenant
https://www.ancient-origins.net/history-famous-people/king-s-drops-0017023
https://en.wikipedia.org/wiki/Battle_of_Bothwell_Bridge
https://drmarkjardine.wordpress.com/2020/06/28/the-wigtown-martyrs-touching-the-void-between-the-reprieve-and-execution-in-1685-history-scotland/
https://www.scotsman.com/whats-on/arts-and-entertainment/wigtown-martyrs-drowned-disobeying-king-600875
https://reformationhistory.org/twomargarets.html
https://www.scottish-places.info/towns/townfirst24701.html
https://drmarkjardine.wordpress.com/category/by-placename/glenvernoch/
https://www.geni.com/people/Gilbert-Wilson-of-Glenvernoch-Parish-of-Penninghame-Scotland/6000000040371360794
https://andyhemingway.wordpress.com/2018/05/13/the-wigtown-martyrs/
https://mydailyartdisplay.uk/2011/07/13/
https://www.britainexpress.com/scotland/Dumfries-Galloway/properties/wigtown-martyrs.htm

Books

History Vindicated in the case of The Wigtown Martyrs,

Rev Archibald Stewart, 1869
The Persecutions in Scotland 1603-1685

People

Andy Hemingway
http://darkgalloway.wordpress.com/

Harvey Mayson
EcoArts (@ecoartsuk) | Instagram

Temple Woman Publishing
www.templewomanpublishing.com

About the Author

Lindsay Banks is a seasoned author, having penned five books including the award-winning "A Gentle Hug for the Soul," spiritual memoir "Awaken Your Soul," and "The Semi Offgrid Journey."

Lindsay is currently writing her sixth book.

To contact Lindsay, please visit:

www.lindsaybanks.uk
www.instagram.com/lindsaybanks_templewoman
www.facebook.com/lindsaybanks
www.twitter.com/lindsaybanks
www.youtube.com/lindsaybanks